Dreams Come True

By: Amanda Lopez

Copyright © 2018 by DesignWrite

All rights reserved. Except as permitted by the Copyright Act of 1976, no part of this book may be reproduced or transmitted in any form or by any means, electronic or mechanical, including photocopying, recording, or by an information storage and retrieval system without permission in writing from the publisher.

For information, contact:
DesignWrite
124 North Cottage Road
Sterling, Virginia 20164

For worldwide distribution.

ISBN: 978-1986621267
Printed in the United States of America
Amazon Publishing, www.CreateSpace.com

In Gratitude

This book is dedicated to Mom and Dad.
Thanks for believing in me.

As a Potentialist, my mom dared to dream big.
She taught me how to listen to the Universe,
co-create miracles, and love myself.

My dad's successful careers in business
and the military became a model for a joyful,
abundant life—as both a follower and a leader.

And thanks to all of you, wonderful dreamers,
for making this book a #1 best seller.
This is my dream come true.

Table of Contents

Dare to Dream	1
1. Test Drive	3
2. Getting Unstuck	5
3. Sleep Better	7
4. Taking Flight	9
5. Mountain Magic	11
Follow Your Bliss	13
6. Find Your Inner Calm	15
7. Change the World	17
8. Bigger	19
9. Set Yourself Free	21
Unfold Your Life	23
10. She	25
11. Gotta Try It	27
12. You've Changed	29
Manifest Your Vision	31
13. Before You Die	33
14. Do More	35
15. For Dramatic Effect	37
16. Enjoy Everything	39
17. Out of This World	41
Dreams Come True	43
18. A Bigger Bucket List	45
19. A Sight to See	47
20. Patriotic Spirit	49
21. Multiracial in America	51
22. Creature Comfort Zone	53

Dare to Dream

What is your true calling? Is your sixth sense driving you forward?
What's in the way of getting exactly what you want?

Dare to dream huge, delicious dreams that scare you. Write down that
brilliant idea, listen to your inspiration, and trust your intuition.
Feel that new dream life pulling you toward it like a magnet.

We all face challenges, doubts, naysayers, and creative blocks.
Support the positive instead. Celebrate each dream spark,
creative impulse, and synchronistic event as one of life's little miracles.

Enjoy each moment of your dream journey. Your dream was always
meant to be; it is simply waiting for your beliefs to catch up.

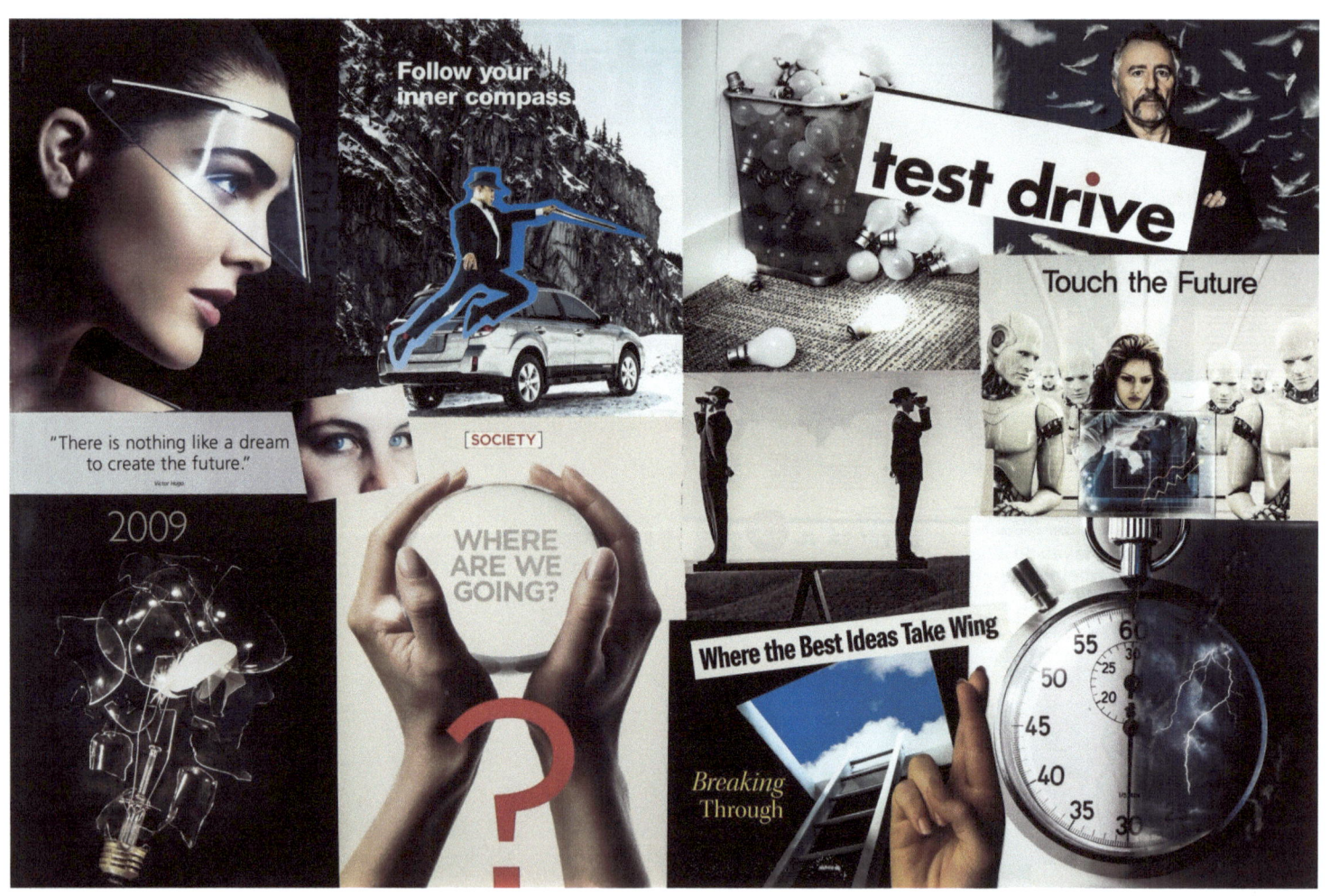

"Test Drive" (2014)

1. "Dare to live the life you have dreamed for yourself. Go forward and make your dreams come true."
~ Ralph Waldo Emerson

2. "When you have a dream, you've got to grab it and never let go."
~ Carol Burnett

3. "A goal is a dream with a deadline."
~ Napoleon Hill

4. "All our dreams can come true, if we have the courage to pursue them."
~ Walt Disney

5. "I tell people I'm too stupid to know what's impossible. I have ridiculously large dreams, and half the time they come true."
~ Debi Thomas

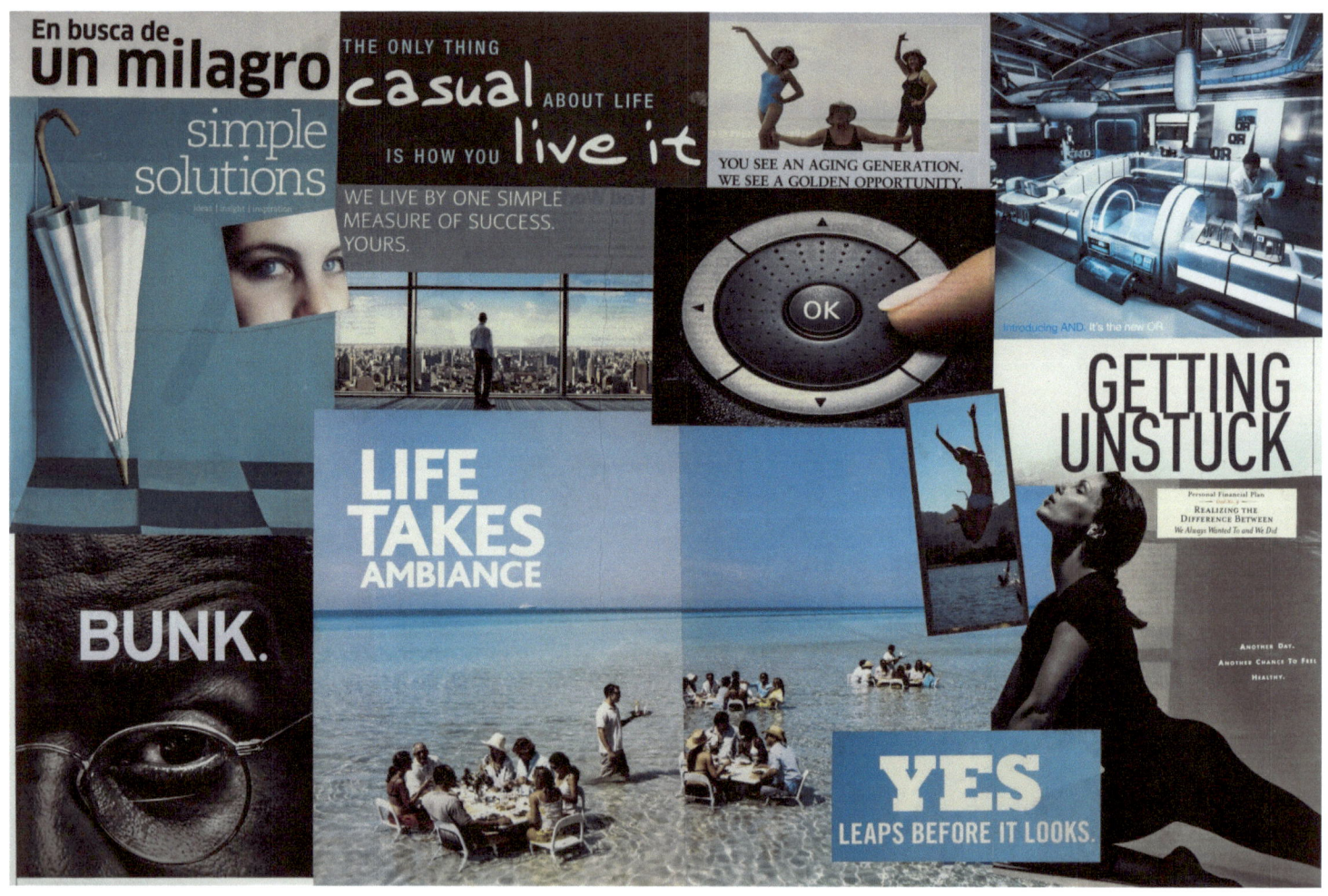

"Getting Unstuck" (2014)

6. "All the things one has forgotten
scream for help in dreams."

~ Elias Canetti

7. "You see things; and you say, Why?
But I dream things that never were;
and I say, Why not?"

~ George Bernard Shaw

8. "The inability to open up is what blocks trust,
and blocked trust is the reason for blighted dreams."

~ Elizabeth Gilbert

9. "People are dream killers. You've got to be careful who
you give emotional access to."

~ Tyrese Gibson

10. "In your heart, keep one still secret spot where
dreams may go and be sheltered so they may thrive and grow."

~ Louise Driscoll

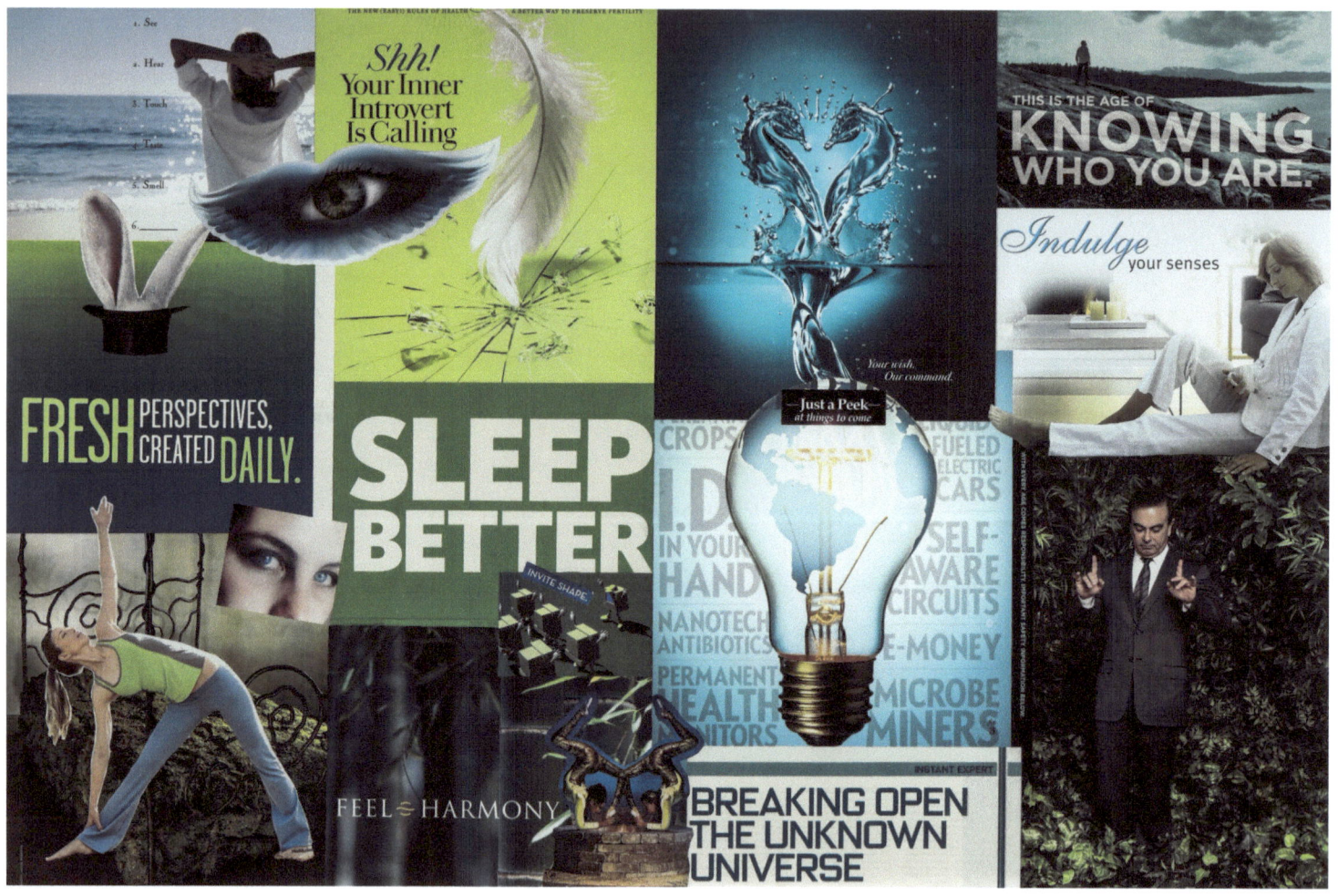

"Sleep Better" (2014)

11. "In bed my real love has always been
the sleep that rescued me by allowing me to dream."

~ Luigi Pirandello

12. "Within our dreams and aspirations
we find our opportunities."

~ Sue Ebaugh

13. "Dreams are like stars…you may never touch them,
but if you follow them they will lead you to your destiny."

~ Liam Payne

14. "It takes a person who is wide awake
to make his dream come true."

~ Roger Ward Babson

15. "Dreams are useful because they are free."

~ Ernesto Sabato

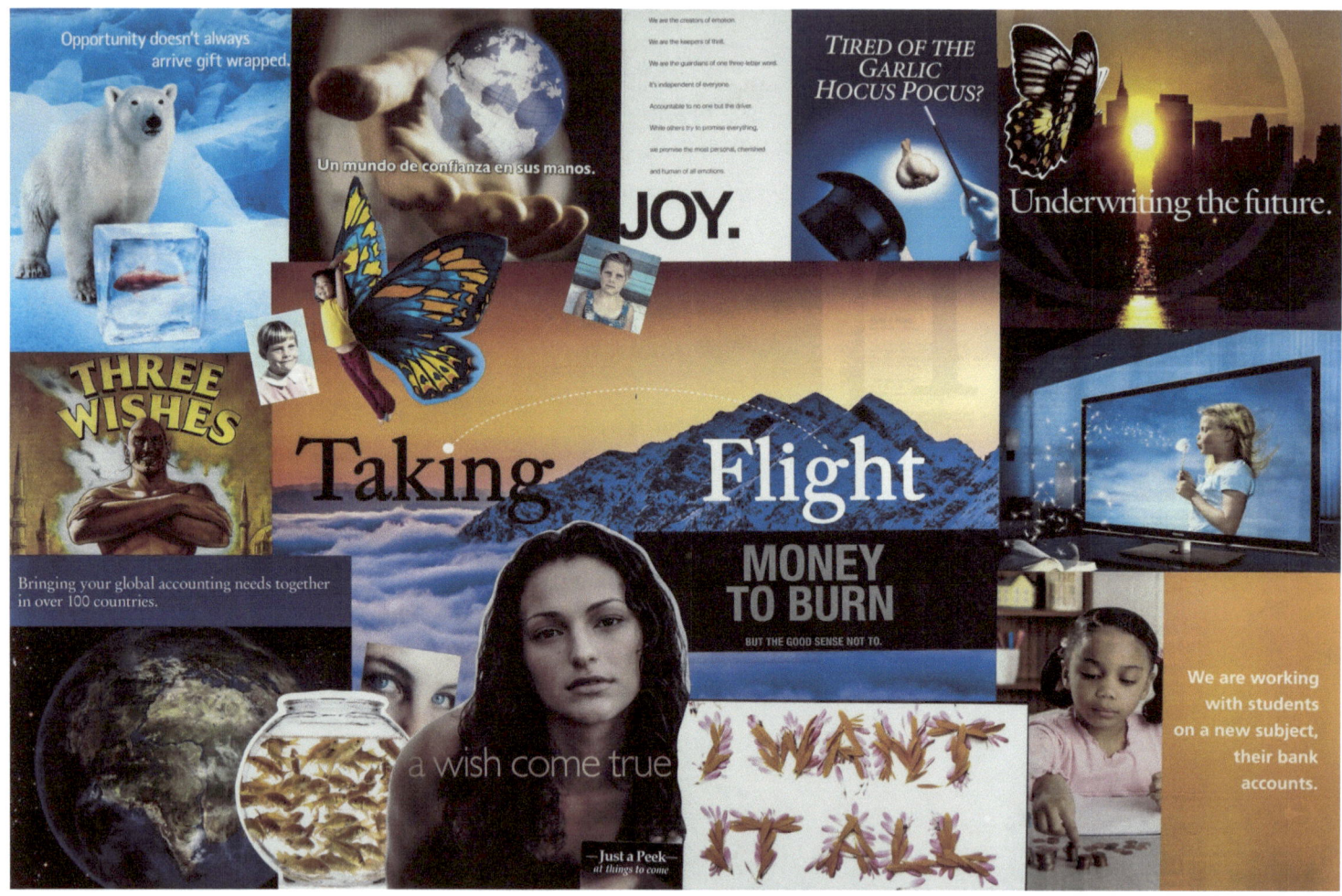

"Taking Flight" (2014)

16. "Hope is a waking dream."

~ Aristotle

17. "To the degree we're not living our dreams, our comfort zone has more control of us than we have over ourselves."

~ Peter McWilliams

18. "Living in dreams of yesterday, we find ourselves still dreaming of impossible future conquests."

~ Charles Lindbergh

19. "You are never too old to set another goal or to dream a new dream."

~ C.S. Lewis

20. "Trust in dreams, for in them is hidden the gate to eternity."

~ Kahlil Gibran

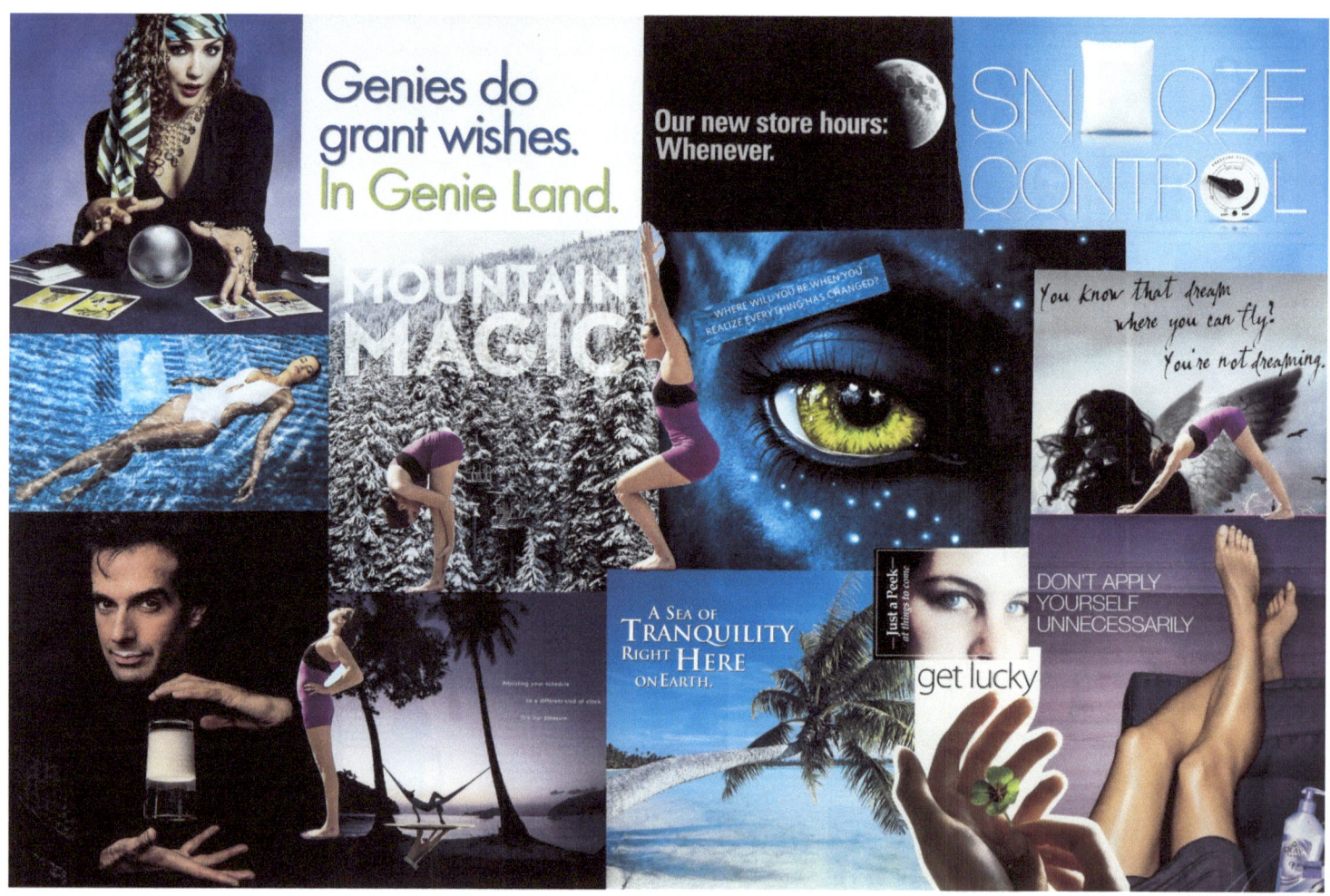

"Mountain Magic" (2011)

21. "It's the possibility of having a dream come true that makes life interesting."

~ Paulo Coelho

22. "Dreams are today's answers to tomorrow's questions."

~ Edgar Cayce

23. "If one dream should fall and break into a thousand pieces, never be afraid to pick one of those pieces up and begin again."

~ Flavia Weedn

24. "You block your dream when you allow your fear to grow bigger than your faith."

~ Mary Manin Morrissey

25. "If the dream is big enough the facts don't matter."

~ Dexter Yager

Follow Your Bliss

Are you living the life you dreamed? Do you look forward to your day?
With only 24 hours to live, what would you be doing, with whom?

Listening to your inner voice reveals new avenues to explore.
If you've found something that gives your life meaning, pursue it.
If you've discovered your life purpose, live it with intention and gusto.

Follow your bliss, write down those compliments, feel that joy,
and watch happiness spread like a wildfire whenever you smile.
Make a daily gratitude list and applaud your achievements.

Feel energized doing what you love. Invest in here and now.
Giggle, hug, and smell those roses. Find who you have not yet become.

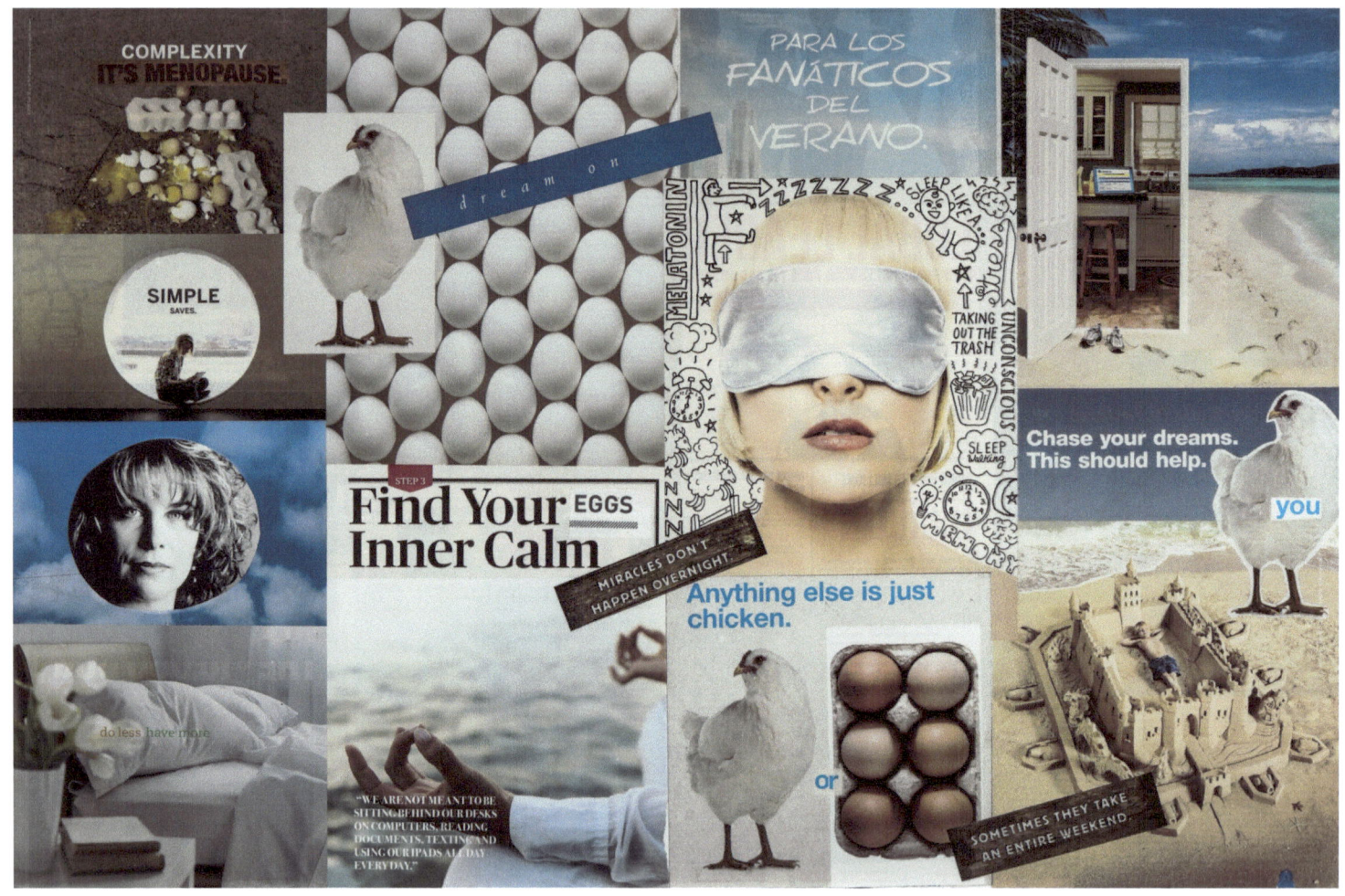

"Find Your Inner Calm" (2016)

26. "The only thing that will stop you
from fulfilling your dreams is you."

~ Tom Bradley

27. "Your vision will become clear only when you can look into your own heart. Who looks outside, dreams; who looks inside, awakens."

~ Carl Jung

28. "Dreams are the seedlings of realities."

~ James Allen

29. "Dreams are only thoughts you didn't
have time to think about during the day."

~ Anonymous

30. "Whatever you can do, or dream you can do,
begin it. Boldness has genius, power, and magic in it."

~ Johann Wolfgang Van Goethe

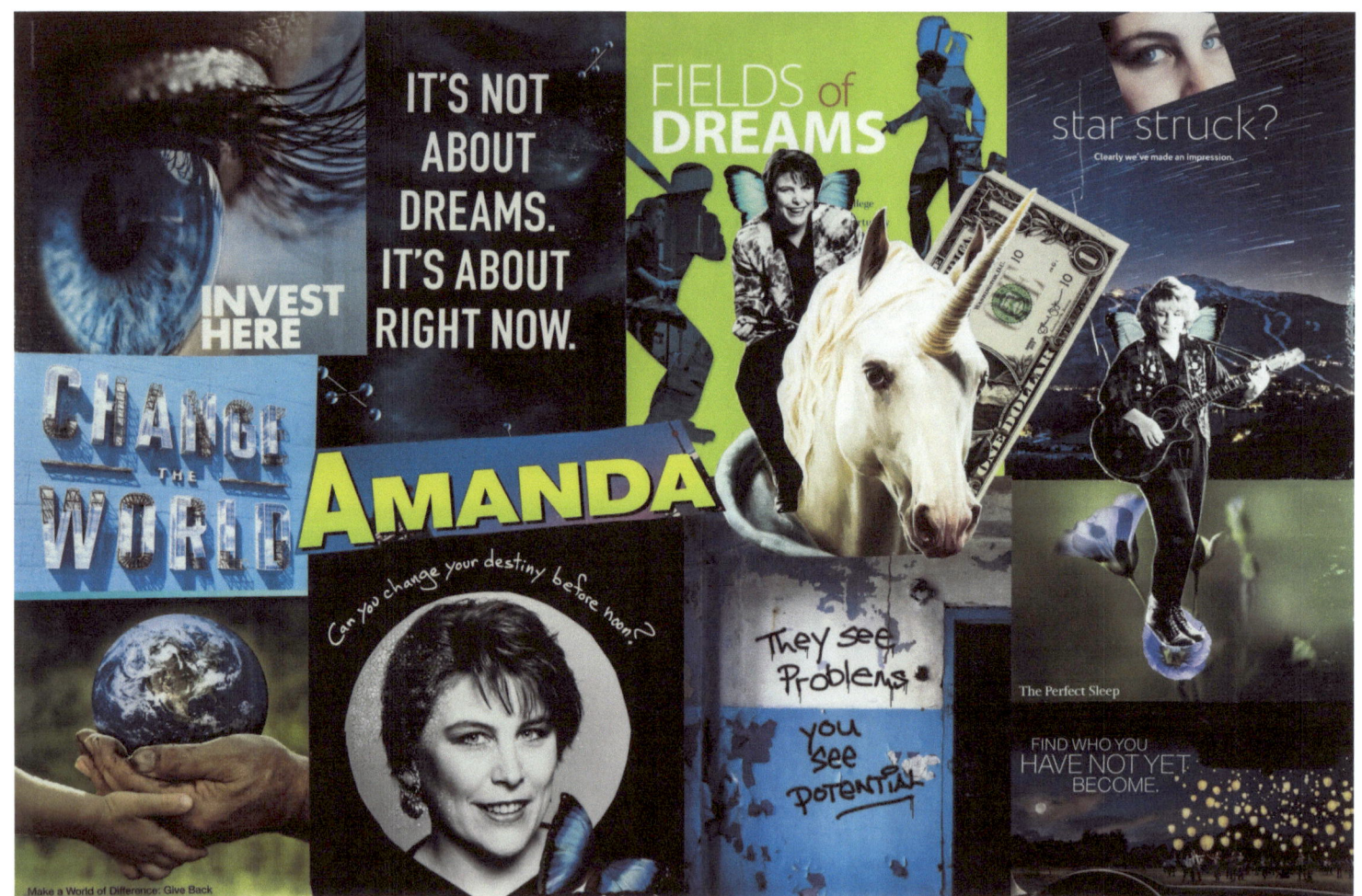

"Change the World" (2016)

31. "If you don't dream big, what's the use of dreaming? If you don't have faith, there's nothing worth believing."

~ Justin Bieber

32. "We all have possibilities we don't know about. We can do things we don't even dream we can do."

~ Dale Carnegie

33. "People who are most afraid of their dreams convince themselves they don't dream at all."

~ John Steinbeck

34. "A #2 pencil and a dream can take you anywhere."

~ Joyce Myers

35. "What one man can do is dream. What one man can do is love. What one man can do is change the world."

~ John Denver

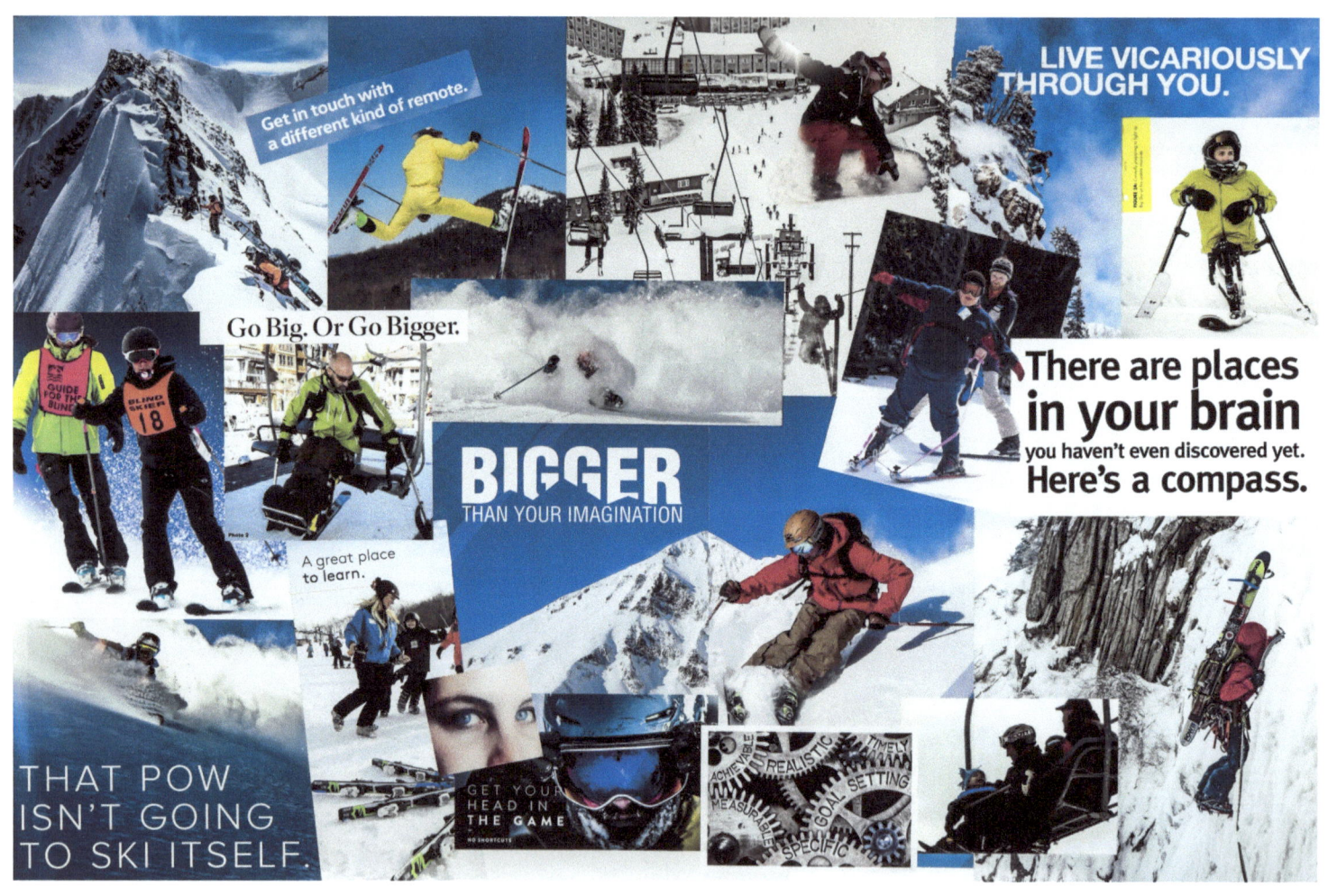

"Bigger" (2018)

36. "Dreams are meaningful only in
the context of the dreamer's life."

~ D. Broadribb

37. "All human beings are also dream beings.
Dreaming ties all mankind together."

~ Jack Kerouac

38. "A dream you dream alone is only a dream.
A dream you dream together is reality."

~ Bella Thorne

39. "It takes a lot of courage to show
your dreams to someone else."

~ Erma Bombeck

40. "If I tell you my dream, you might forget it.
If I act on my dream, perhaps you will remember it,
but if I involve you, it becomes your dream too."

~ Tibetan proverb

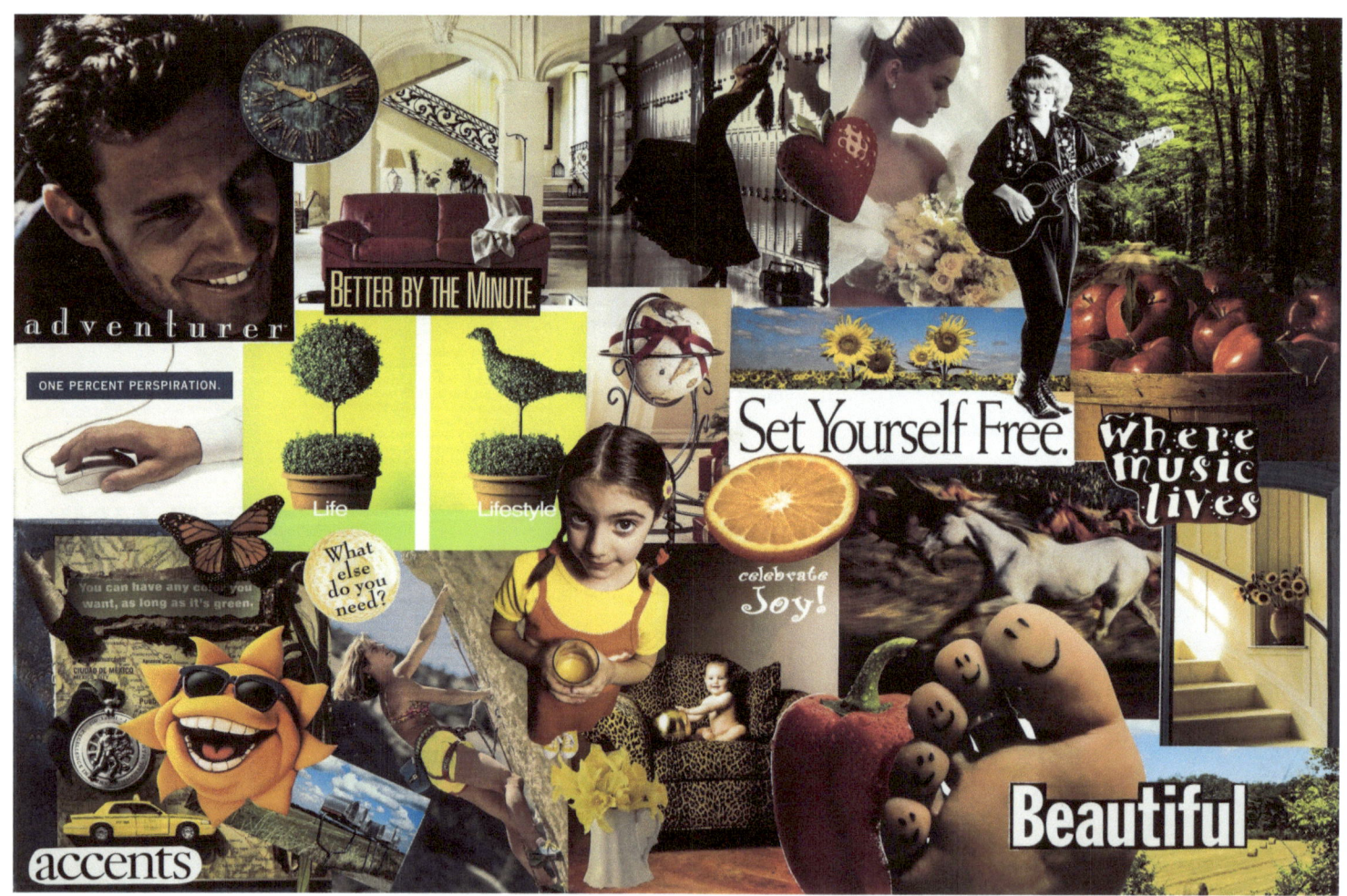

"Set Yourself Free" (1999)

41. "If your actions inspire others to dream more,
learn more, do more and become more, you are a leader."

~ John Quincy Adams

42. "Yes, you can be a dreamer and a doer too;
if you will remove one word from your vocabulary."

~ Robert H. Schuller

43. "As soon as you can start to pursue a dream,
your life wakes up and everything has meaning."

~ Barbara Sher

44. "A vision without a task is just a dream.
A task without a vision is just a job.
A vision with a task can change the world."

~ Edward Mills

45. "Dream as if you'll live forever.
Live as if you'll die today."

~ James Dean

Unfold Your Life

Where will you be when you realize that everything has changed?
Do you like the self-actualized dreamer you've become?

You can refine your dream, or change it completely—your choice.
The space between your dream and reality requires conviction and continuous steps in the right direction. The sky is the limit.

As you watch your life unfold, share your dream
with trusted friends, family, and like-minded individuals.
That way, everyone gets to swim in your faith and positive results.

When you believe in the beauty of your own dream,
the future is bright and change is good.

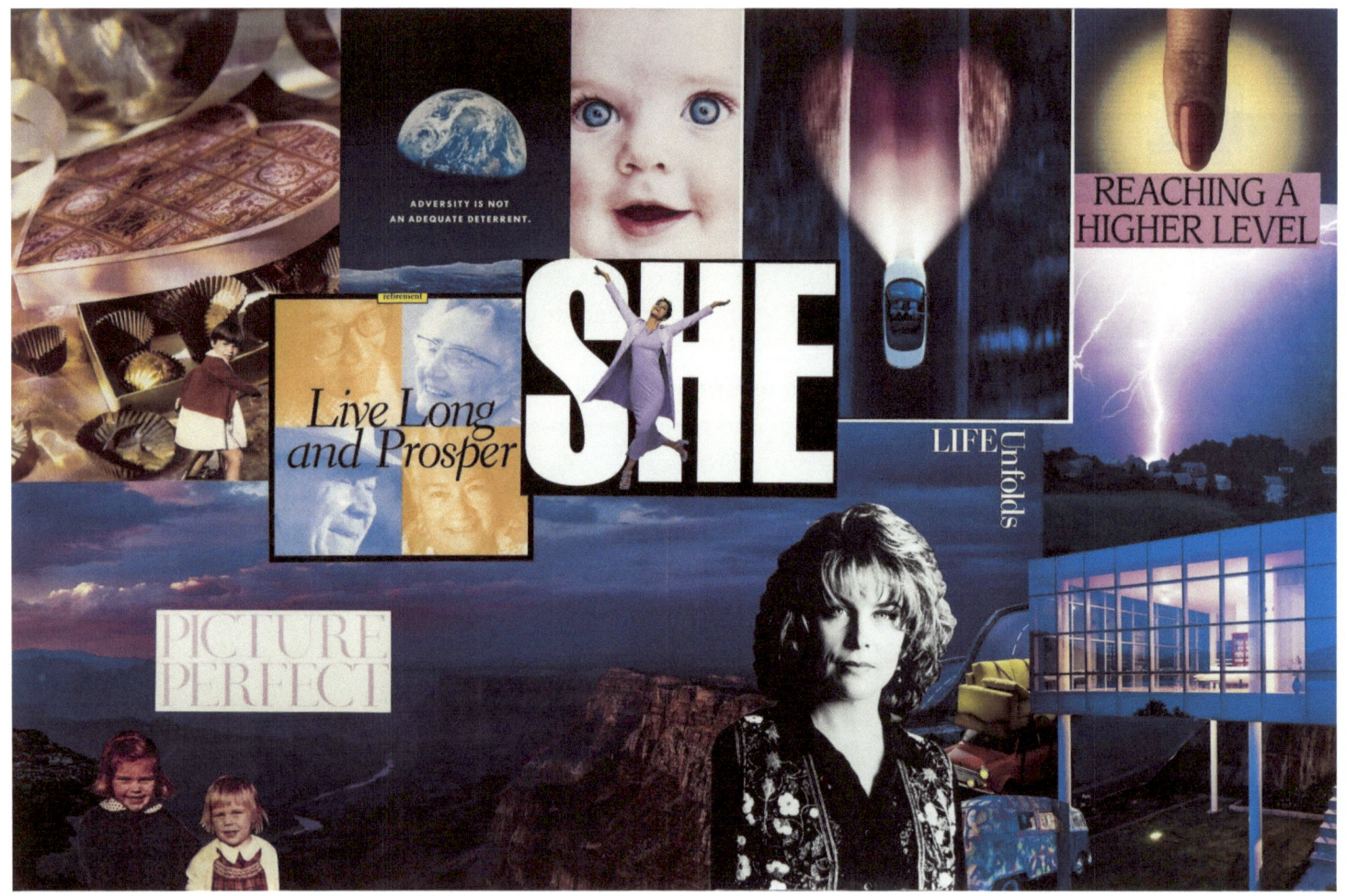

"She" (2003)

46. "People need dreams; there's as much nourishment in 'em as food."

~ Dorothy Gilman

47. "To hope and dream is not to ignore the practical. It is to dress it in colors and rainbows."

~ Anne Wilson Schaef

48. "For my part I know nothing with any certainty, but the sight of the stars makes me dream."

~ Vincent Van Gogh

49. "The future belongs to those who believe in the beauty of their dreams."

~ Eleanor Roosevelt

50. "If a little dreaming is dangerous, the cure for it is not to dream less but to dream more, to dream all the time."

~ Marcel Proust

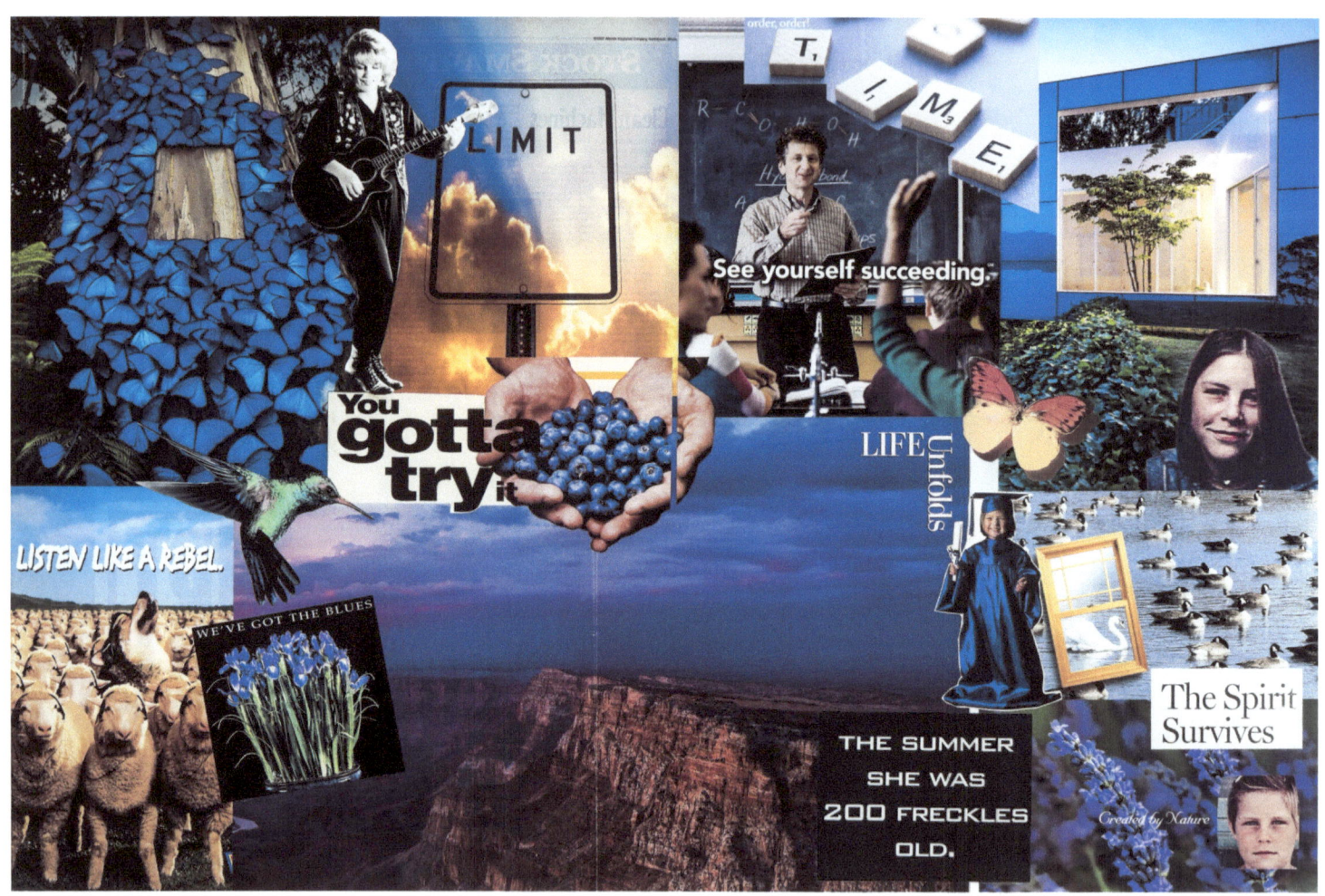

"Gotta Try It" (2003)

51. "If you take responsibility for yourself, you will develop a hunger to accomplish your dreams."

~ Les Brown

52. "We can't achieve our wildest dreams by remaining who we are."

~ John C. Maxwell

53. "Dreams come true. Without that possibility, nature would not incite us to have them."

~ John Updike

54. "The dream is real, my friends. The failure to realize it is the only unreality."

~ Toni Cade Bambara

55. "Don't be afraid of the space between your dreams and reality. If you can dream it, you can make it so."

~ Belva Davis

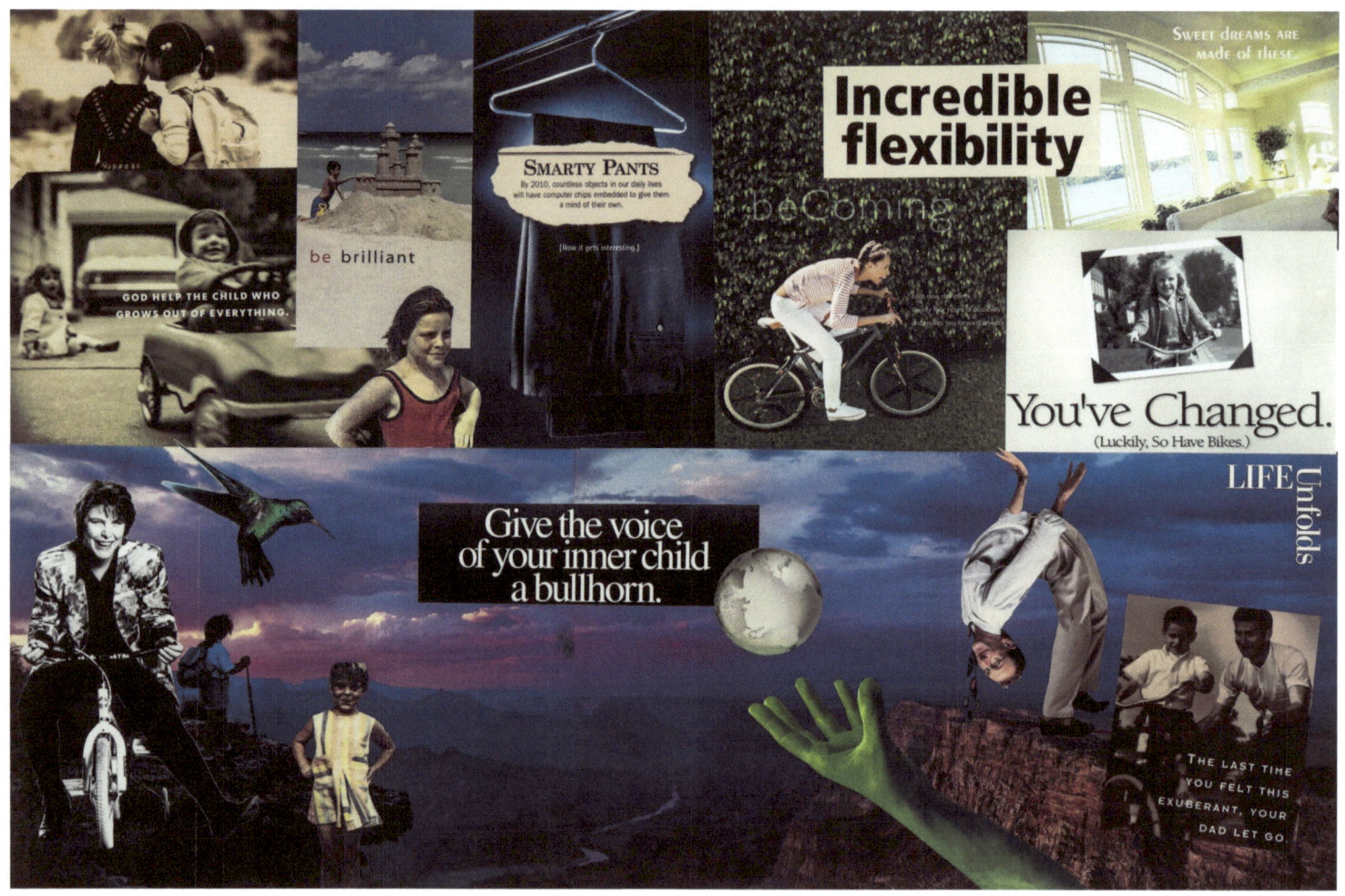

"You've Changed" (2003)

56. "Nothing happens unless first we dream."

~ Carl Sandburg

57. "Awaken your sense, your intuition, your desires. Awaken the parts of yourself that have been sleeping. Life is a dream, and to live it, you must be awake."

~ Rachel Snyder

58. "If you dream only while sleeping you are giving your own possibilities only half measure."

~ Sophia Bedford-Pierce

59. "A dreamer is one who can only find his way by moonlight, and his punishment is that he sees the dawn before the rest of the world."

~ Oscar Wilde

60. "At last the ladder, which had been built slowly, one hope at a time, reached up to the clouds. And the dreamer began to climb."

~ Katherine G. Berry

Manifest Your Vision

Think you're too old to dream big? What are you passionate about? How much time will you take today to help realize your dream?

Learn something new. Aging and the passage of time can limit dreams. Luckily, you can discover a new passion at any age.

Travel through time using dreams to go forward, memories to go backward, and your imagination to go out of this world.

Recognize the significance of your dream. Applaud both your desire, and the belief that you can manifest that desire. Prepare yourself daily to persevere for as long as it takes.

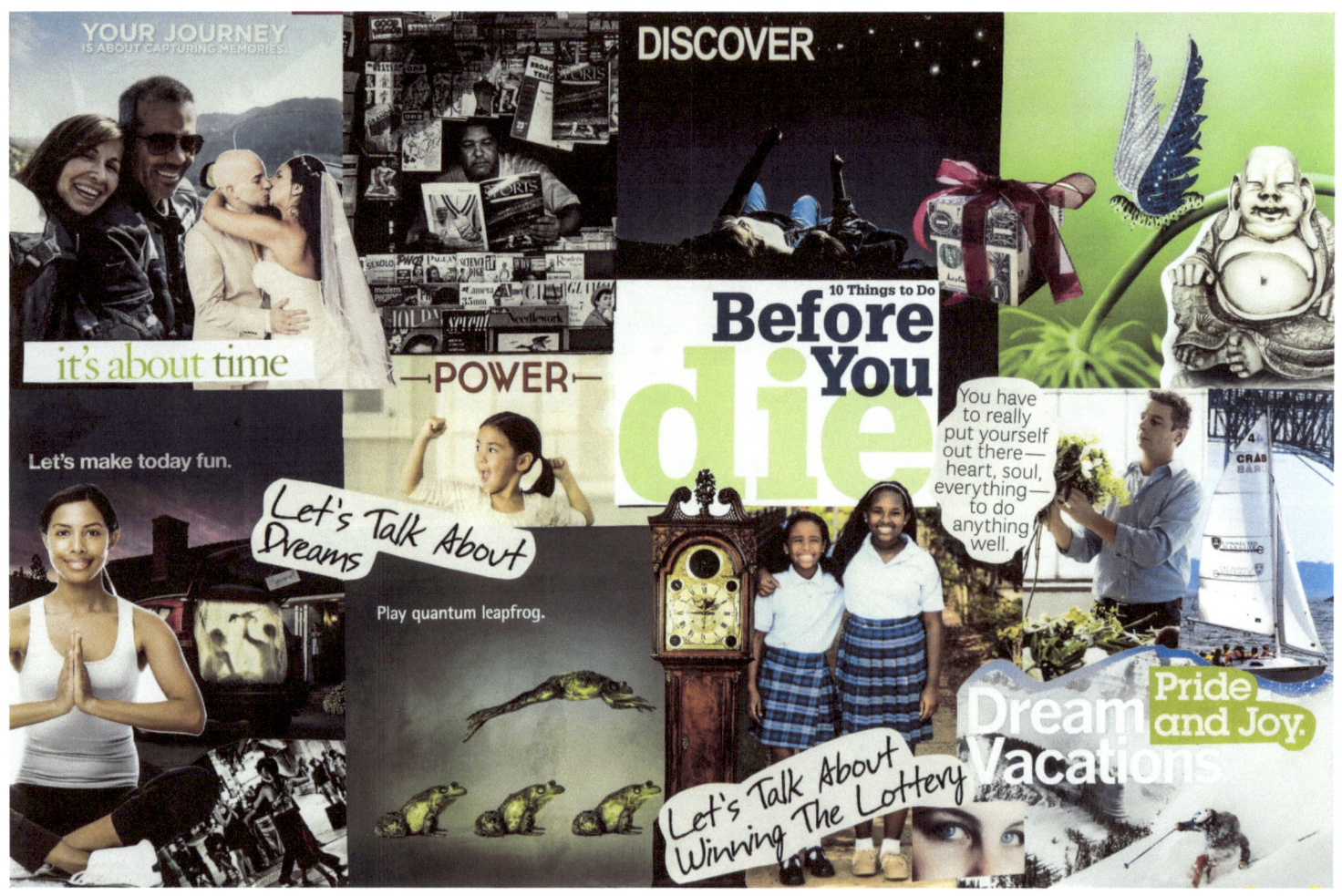

"Before You Die" (2014)

61. "Only as high as I reach can I grow, Only as far as I seek can I go, Only as deep as I look can I see, Only as much as I dream can I be."

~ Karen Ravn

62. "Don't let fear get in the way of your dreams even if your biggest fear is your biggest dream."

~ John Lennon

63. "To accomplish great things, we must not only act, but also dream; not only plan, but also believe."

~ Anatole France

64. "Dreams are illustrations… from the book your soul is writing about you."

~ Marsha Norman

65. "A man is not old until regrets take the place of dreams."

~ John Barrymore

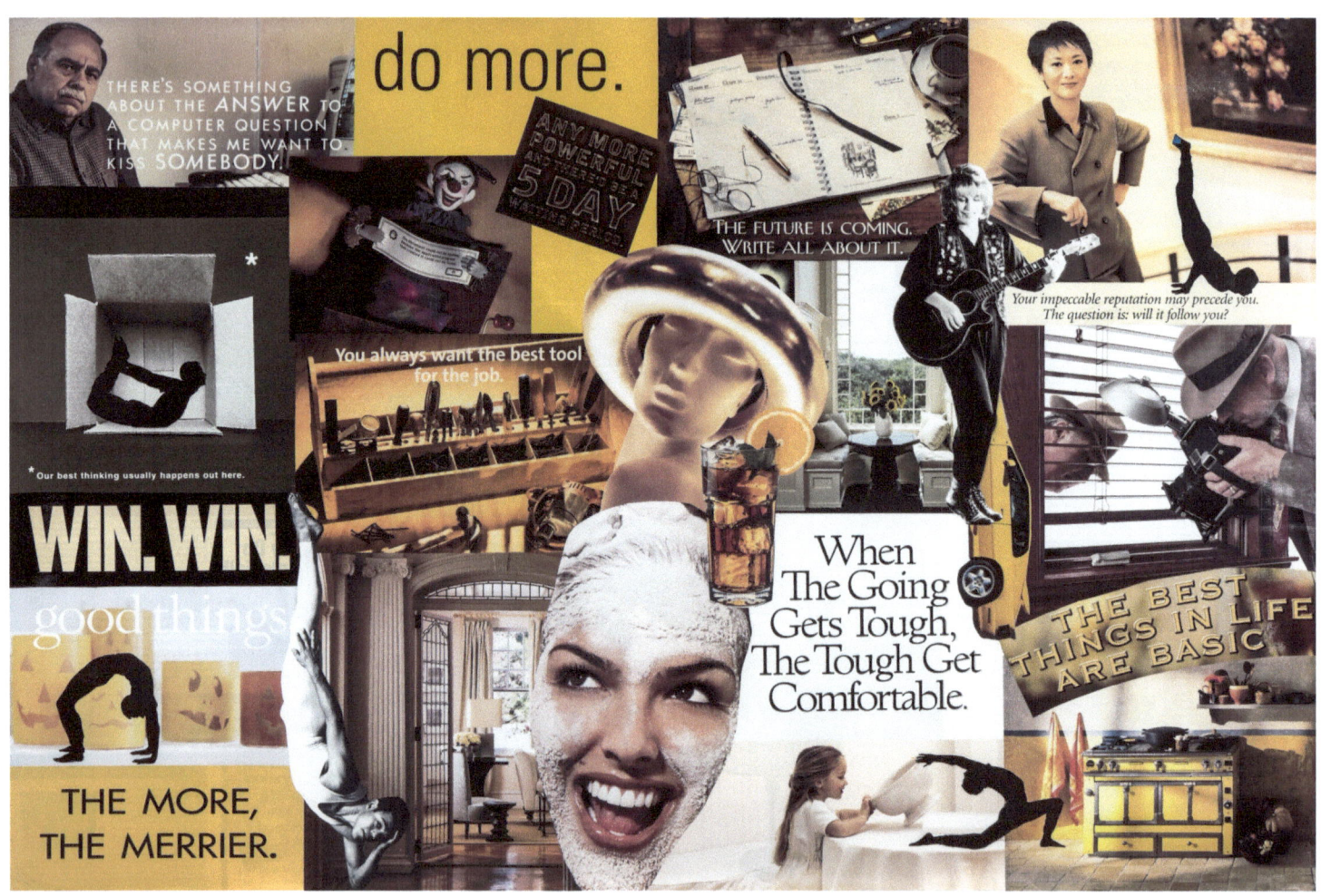

"Do More" (2000)

66. "Some women choose to follow men, and some choose to follow their dreams. If you're wondering which way to go, remember that your career will never wake up and tell you it doesn't love you anymore."
~ Lady Gaga

67. "When our memories outweigh our dreams, we've grown old."
~ Bill Clinton

68. "To fulfill a dream, to be allowed to sweat over lonely labor, to be given a chance to create, is the meat and potatoes of life. The money is the gravy."
~ Bette Davis

69. "Always dream and shoot higher than you know how to. Don't bother just to be better than your contemporaries or predecessors. Try to be better than yourself."
~ William Faulkner

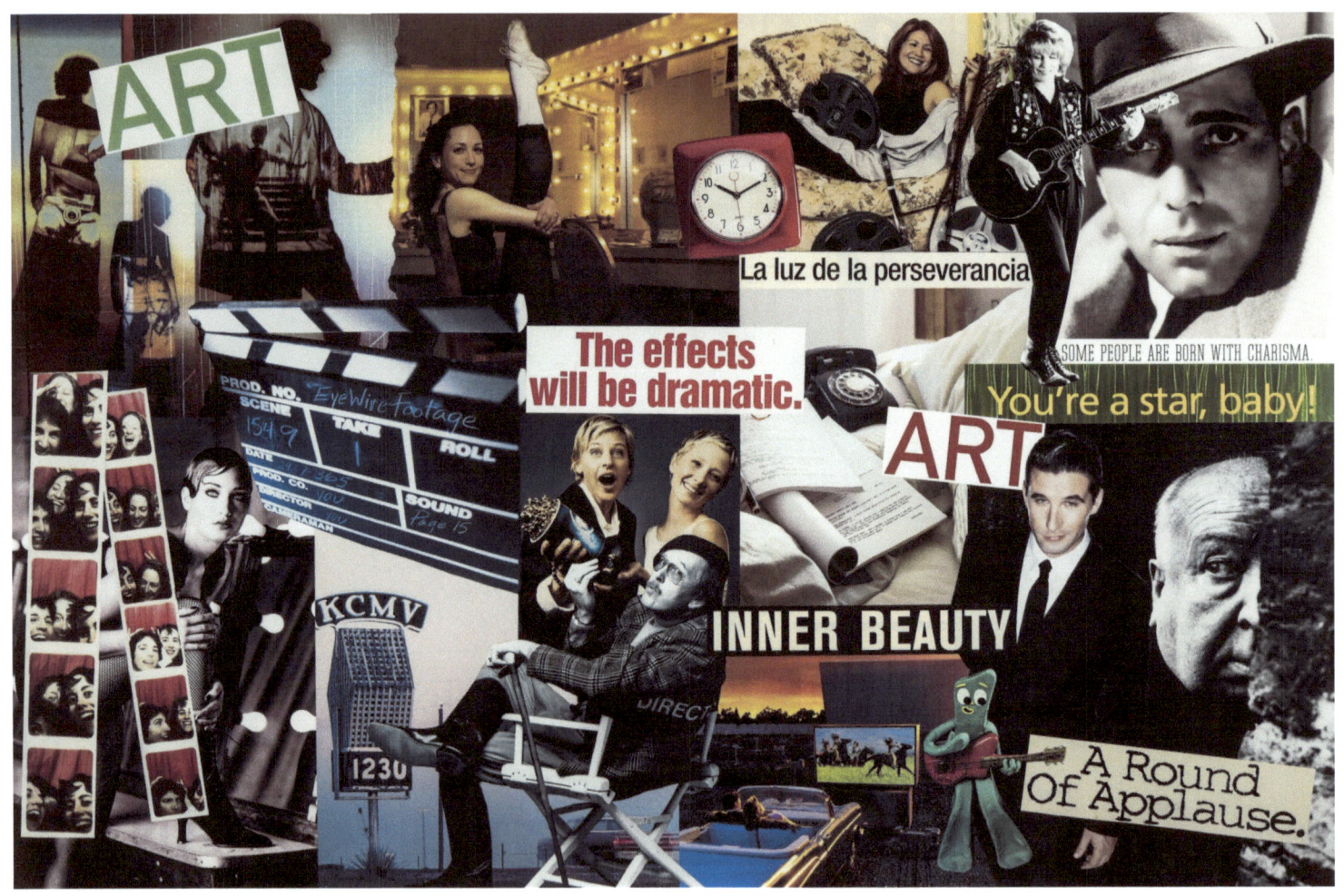

"For Dramatic Effect" (2000)

70. "The flower doesn't dream of the bee.
It blossoms and the bee comes."

~ Mark Nepo

71. "If you're still hanging on to a dead dream
of yesterday—laying flowers on its grave
by the hour—you cannot be planting the
seeds for a new dream to grow today."

~ Joyce Chapman

72. "Dreams are renewable. No matter what
our age or condition, there are still
untapped possibilities within us and
new beauty waiting to be born."

~ Dale E. Turner

73. "The key to realizing a dream is to focus
not on success, but significance—and then,
even the small steps and little victories along
your path will take on greater meaing."

~ Oprah Winfrey

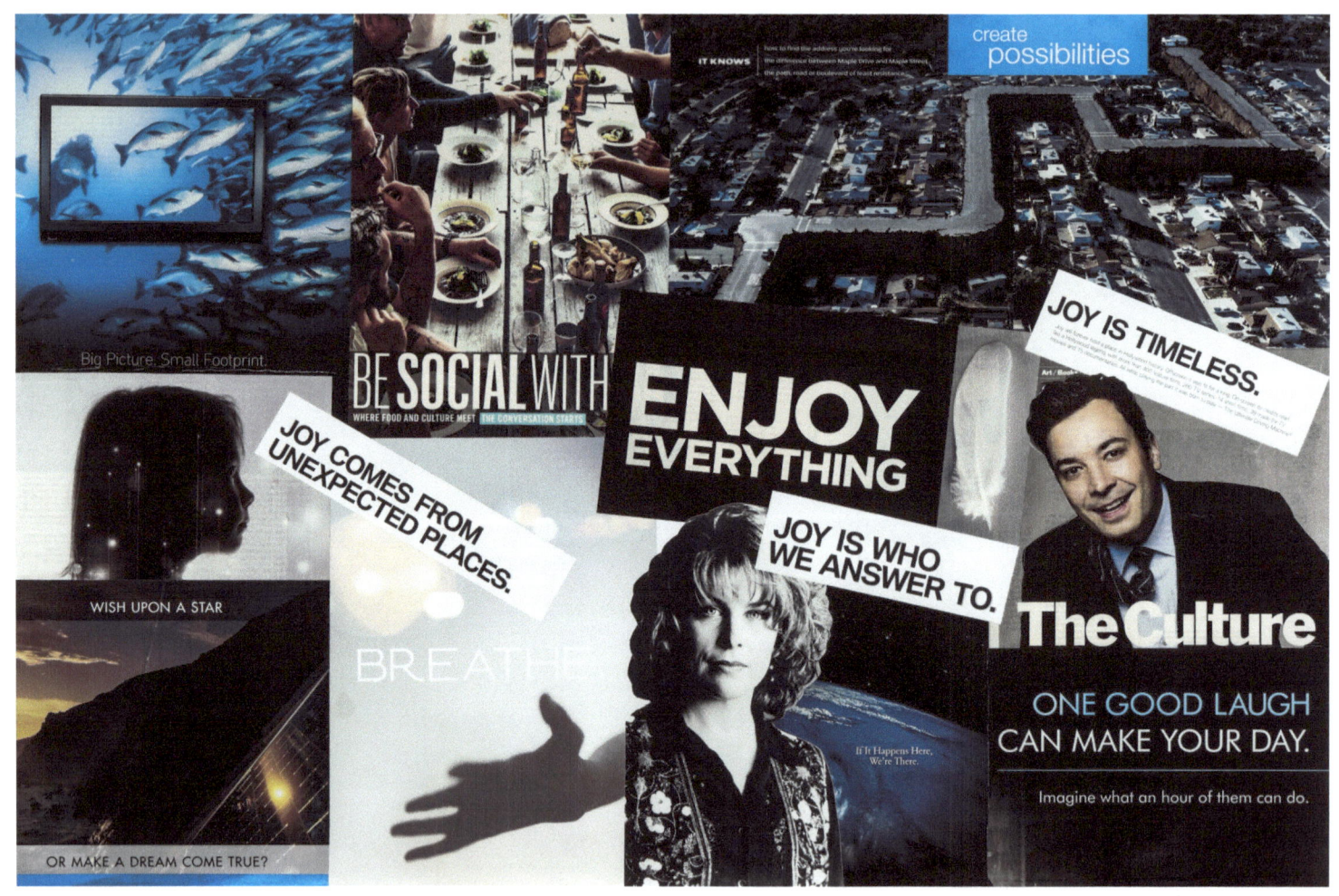

"Enjoy Everything" (2014)

74. "Dream until your dreams come true..."

~ Aerosmith

75. "You are everything that is, your thoughts, your life, your dreams come true. You are everything that you choose to be. You are as unlimited as the endless universe."

~ Shad Helmstetter

76. "Those who dream by day are cognizant of many things that escape those who dream only at night."

~ Edgar Allan Poe

77. "I slept and I dreamed that life is all joy. I woke and I saw that life is all service. I served and I saw that service is joy."

~ Kahlil Gibran

78. "Spiritual awakening is awakening from the dream of thought."

~ Eckhart Tolle

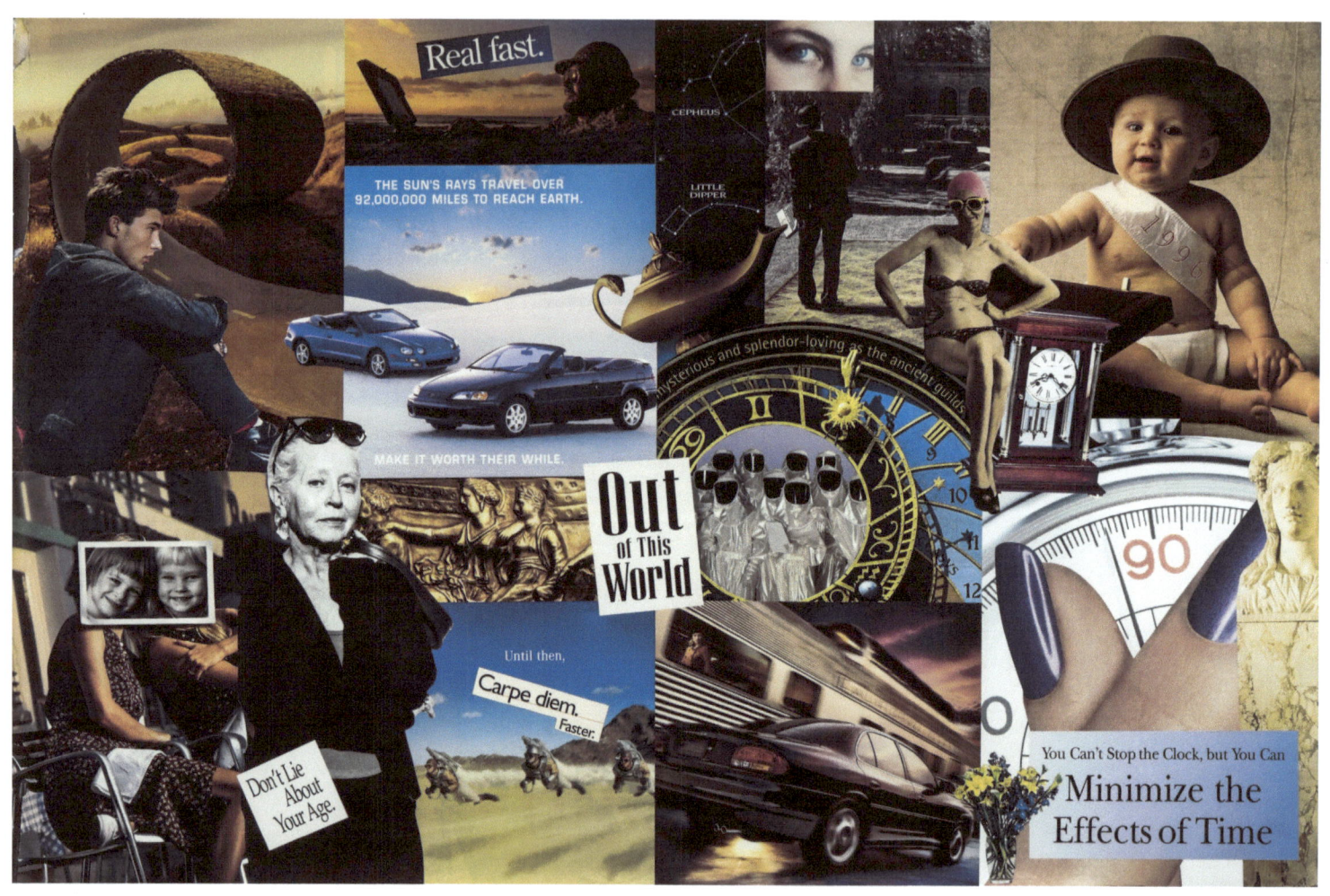

"Out of This World" (2000)

79. "The timeless in you is aware of timelessness and knows that yesterday is but today's memory, and tomorrow is today's dream."

~ Kahlil Gibran

80. "We all have our time machines, don't we. Those that take us back are memories...And those that carry us forward, are dreams."

~ H.G. Wells

81. "I find out a lot about myself by sleeping. Dreams, they are who I am when I'm too tired to be me."

~ Jarod Kintz

82. "The only difference between hopes and dreams is a good night's sleep."

~ Amanda Lopez

83. "Doubt kills more dreams than failure ever will."

~ Suzy Kassem

Dreams Come True

Which of your dreams have already come true?
Where to next? What are you waiting for?

Sweat, determination, and hard work will make your garden grow.
Cultivate a bumper crop of ideas beyond your wildest dreams.

Recognize those extraordinary details appearing each and every day.
The dream journey itself brings as much joy as the realized dream.

Reach far beyond what you know is possible today.
Adversity will only make you strive harder.

You have the power to change the world,
and make your dreams come true.

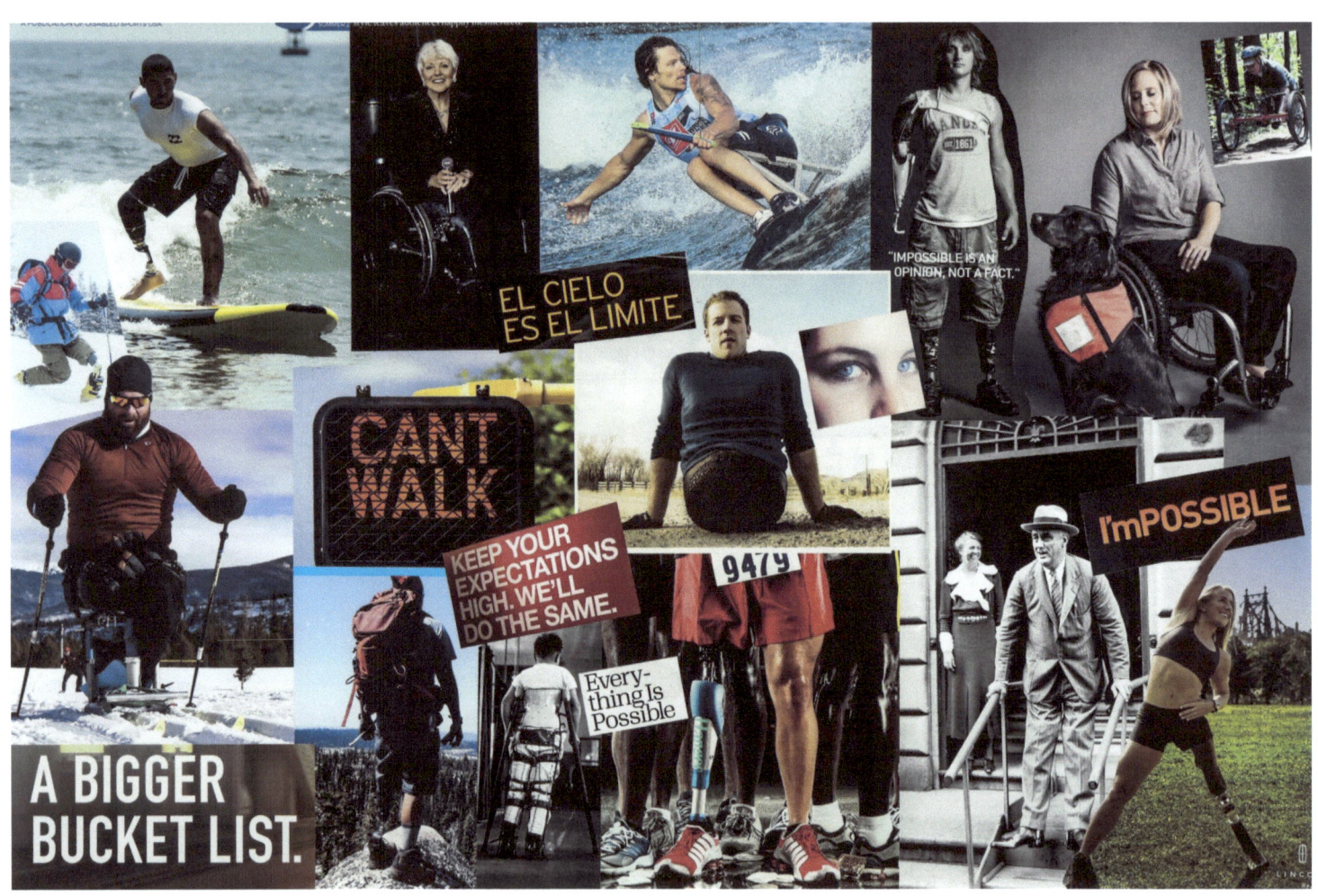

"A Bigger Bucket List" (2017)

84. "Giving up is easy; anyone can do it. To continue fighting for your dream is what makes you a success."

~ Gonzalo Arzuaga

85. "Champions aren't made in the gyms. Champions are made from something they have deep inside them--a desire, a dream, a vision."

~ Muhammad Ali

86. "Go, young man, follow your dream, and if you do not find the happiness that you seek, at any rate you will have had the happiness of seeking it."

~ Andrew Lang

87. "If you've forgotten why life's worth living, follow your bliss. If you find others on your same path, dare to dream bigger together."

~ Amanda Lopez

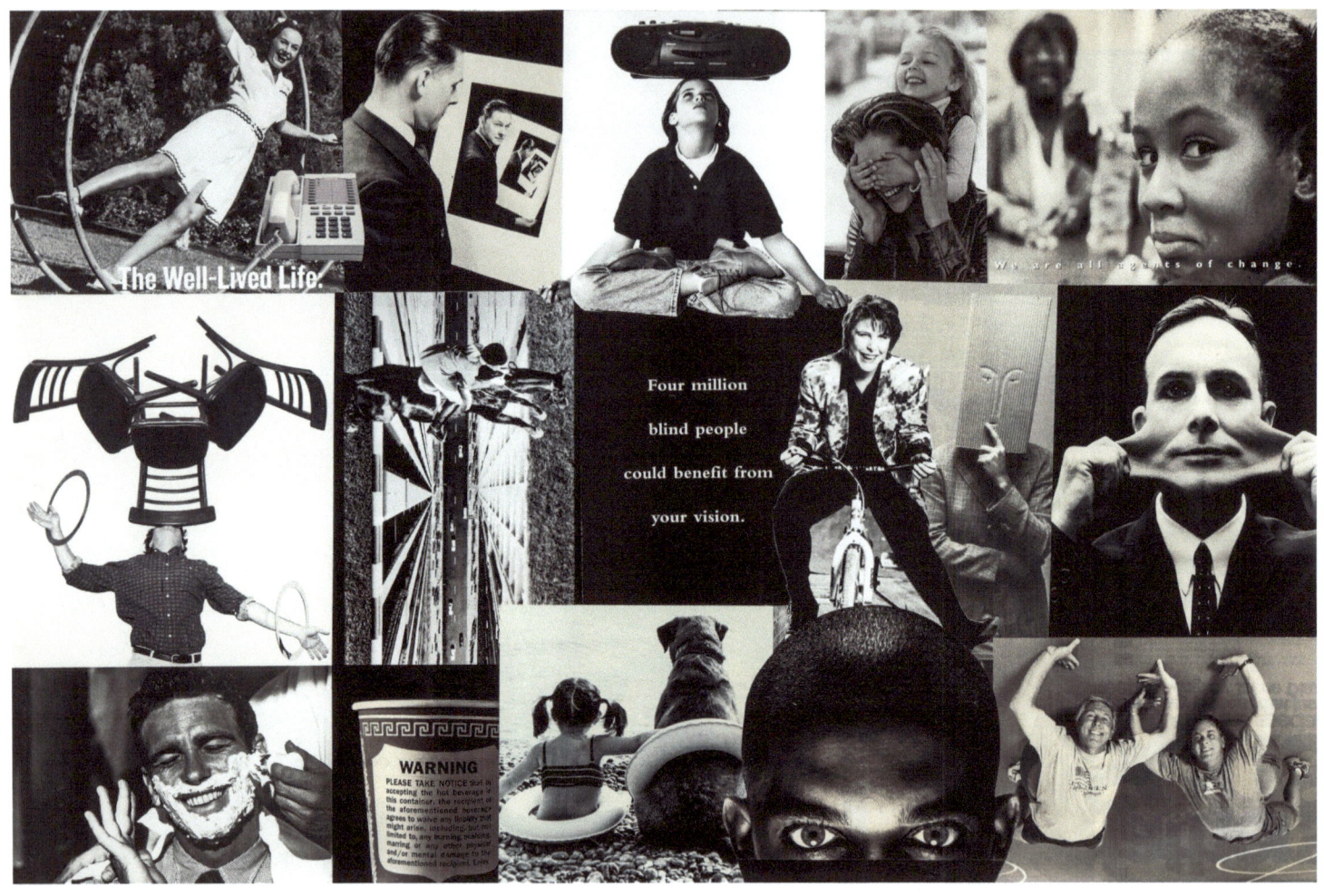

"A Sight to See" (2008)

88. "I used to dream about escaping my ordinary life, but my life was never ordinary. I had simply failed to notice how extraordinary it was."

~ Ransom Riggs

89. "Meditation is wakeful dreaming. It tills the soil for planting seeds; and opens my soul to a universe of potential."

~ Amanda Lopez

90. "Cherish your visions and your dreams as they are the children of your soul; the blueprint of your ultimate achievements."

~ Napoleon Hill

91. "The ability to dream is all I have to give. That is my responsibility; that is my burden. And even I grow tired."

~ Harlan Ellison

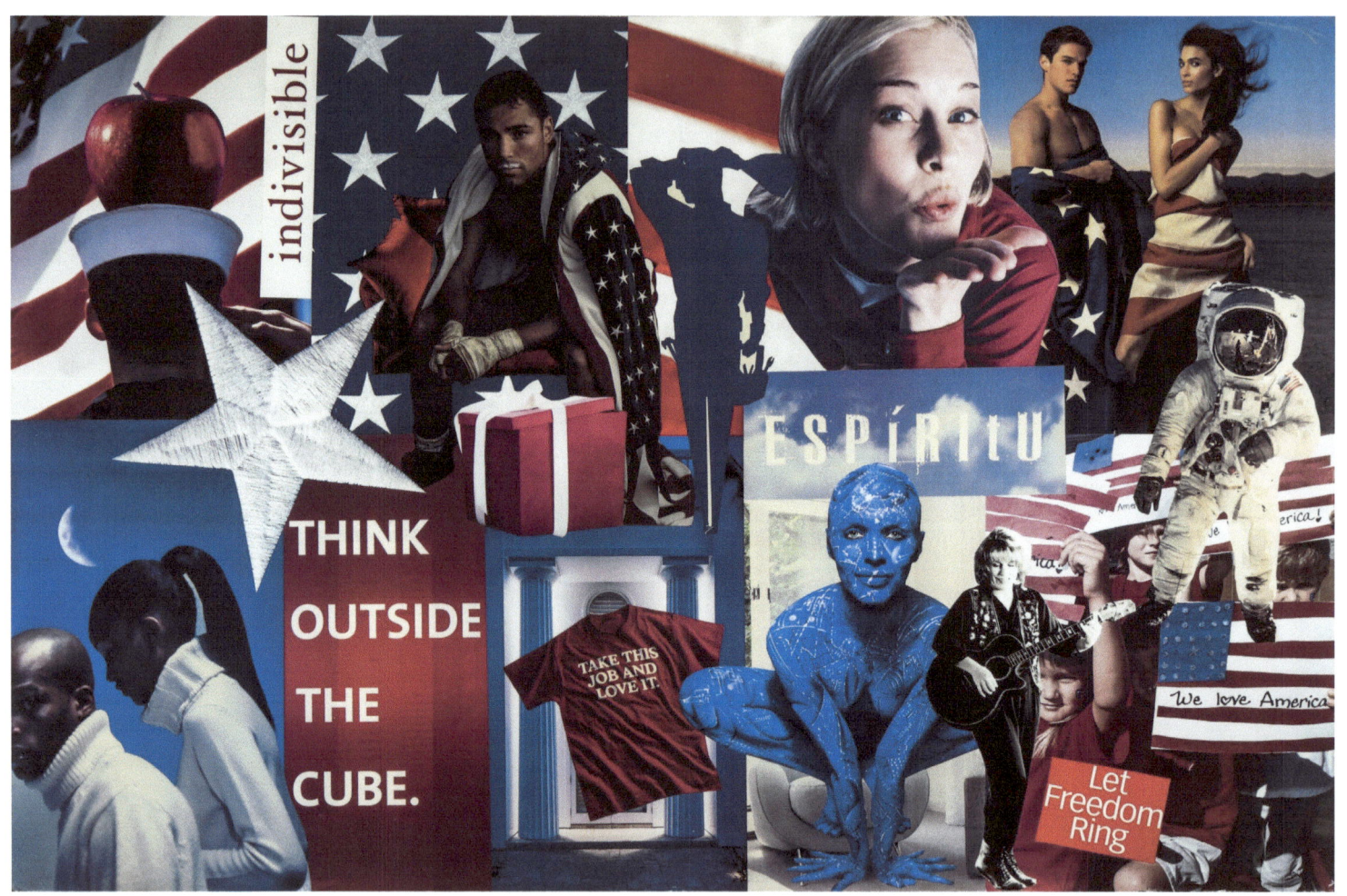

"Patriotic Spirit" (2002)

92. "Your dream doesn't have an expiration date.
Take a deep breath and try again."

~ KT Witten

93. "A dream doesn't become reality through magic;
it takes sweat, determination and hard work."

~ Colin Powell

94. "In a world filled with hate, we must still dare to hope.
In a world filled with anger, we must still dare to comfort.
In a world filled with despair, we must still dare to dream.
And in a world filled with distrust, we must still dare to believe."

~ Michael Jackson

95. "Miracles are like pimples, because once you start looking for
them you find more than you ever dreamed you'd see."

~ Daniel Handler

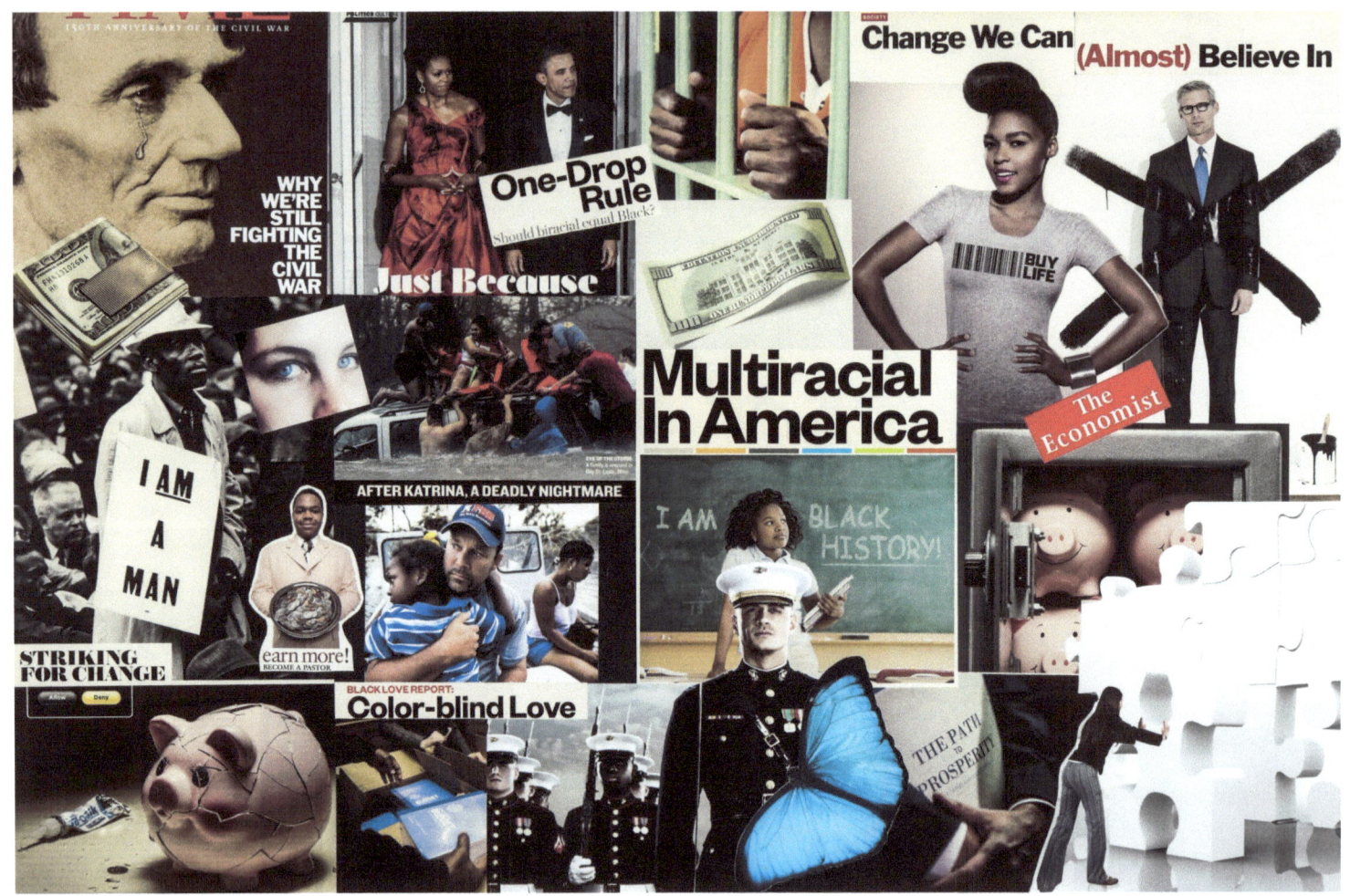

"Multiracial in America" (2012)

96. "I have no fear of death. It just means dreaming in silence: a dream that lasts for eternity."

~ Rouén D. E. Robinson

97. "You're never given a dream without also being given the power to make it true."

~ Richard Bach

98. "Every great dream begins with a dreamer. Always remember, you have within you the strength, the patience, and the passion to reach for the stars to change the world."

~ Harriet Tubman

99. "Life is an opportunity, benefit from it. Life is beauty, admire it. Life is a dream, realize it."

~ Mother Teresa

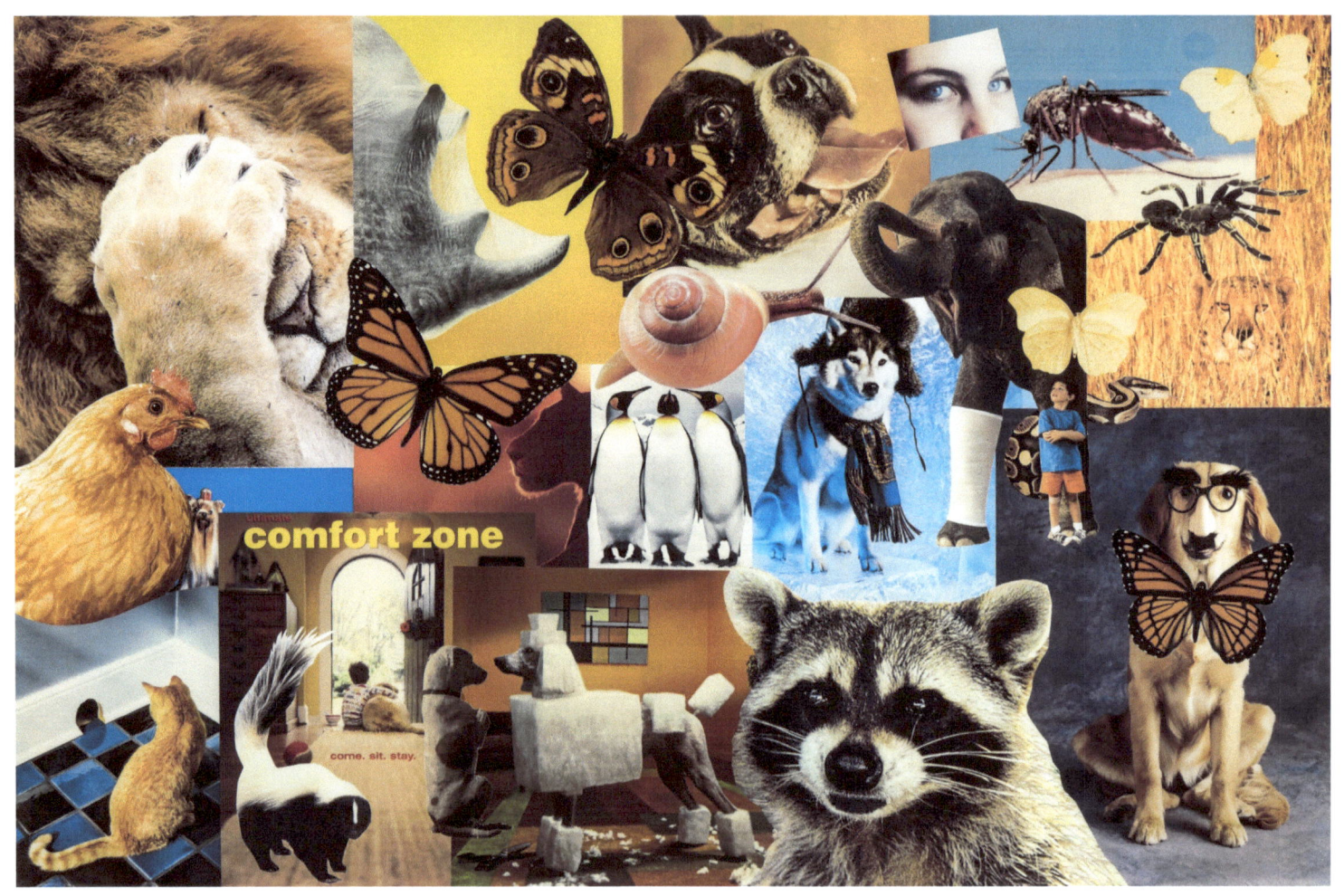

"Creature Comfort Zone" (2005)

100. "Have a dream so big that you cannot achieve it until you grow into the person who can."

~ Thomas Henry Huxley

Glossary

A

John Quincy Adams	21
Aerosmith	39
Muhammad Ali	45
James Allen	15
Anonymous	15
Aristotle	9
Gonzalo Arzuaga	45

B

Roger Ward Babson	7
Richard Bach	51
Toni Cade Bambara	27
John Barrymore	33
Sophia Bedford-Pierce	29
Katherine G. Berry	29
Justin Bieber	17
Erma Bombeck	19
Tom Bradley	15
D. Broadribb	19
Les Brown	27
Carol Burnett	3

C

Elias Canetti	5
Dale Carnegie	17
Edgar Cayce	11
Joyce Chapman	37
Bill Clinton	35
Paulo Coelho	11

D

Belva Davis	27
Bette Davis	35
James Dean	21
John Denver	17
Walt Disney	3
Louise Driscoll	5

E

Sue Ebaugh	7
Harlan Ellison	47
Ralph Waldo Emerson	3

F

William Faulkner	35
Anatole France	33

G

Kahlil Gibran	9,39,41
Tyrese Gibson	5
Elizabeth Gilbert	5
Dorothy Gilman	25

H

Daniel Handler	49
Shad Helmstetter	39
Napoleon Hill	3,47
Thomas Henry Huxley	53

J

Michael Jackson   49
Carl Jung   15

K

Suzy Kassem   41
Jack Kerouac   19
Jarod Kintz   41

L

Lady Gaga   35
Andrew Lang   45
John Lennon   33
C.S. Lewis   9
Charles Lindbergh   9
Amanda Lopez   41, 45, 47

M

John C. Maxwell   27
Peter McWilliams   9
Edward Mills   21
Mary Manin Morrissey   11
Mother Teresa   51
Joyce Myers   17

N

Mark Nepo   37
Marsha Norman   33

P

Liam Payne   7
Luigi Pirandello   7
Edgar Allan Poe   39
Colin Powell   49
Marcel Proust   25

R

Karen Ravn   33
Ransom Riggs   47
Rouén D. E. Robinson   51
Eleanor Roosevelt   25

S

Ernesto Sabato   7
Carl Sandburg   29
Anne Wilson Schaef   25
Robert H. Schuller   21
George Bernard Shaw   5
Barbara Sher   21
Rachel Snyder   29
John Steinbeck   17

T

Tibetan proverb   19
Debi Thomas   3
Bella Thorne   19
Eckhart Tolle   39

Harriet Tubman 51
Dale E. Turner 37

U
John Updike 27

V
Johann Wolfgang Van Goethe 15
Vincent Van Gogh 25

W
Flavia Weedn 11
H.G. Wells 41
Oscar Wilde 29
Oprah Winfrey 37
KT Witten 49

Y
Dexter Yager 11

About the Artist

Amanda Lopez had fun making collages as a kid. She rediscovered them after studying journalism at George Mason University. She now uses collage art as a communication tool—and as a way to help others make their own dreams come true.

Amanda's inspiring journey started with her first dream collage as a singer-songwriter in Nashville, TN. Little did she know that collage art itself would become her future. She continues to make dream collages to envision career changes, celebrate her love life, and discover what her future holds.

In the 1990s, Amanda merged magazine images with similar colors into a single collage. She noted ad campaigns and magazine covers often captured current events and discussion topics, such as war, politics, money, spirituality, and healthcare. This made it easy to choose a collage theme to visually report on the world.

Before laminating, Amanda "signs" each collage by adding a photo of herself. When she looks back at an old collage today, it sometimes helps her solve a puzzle, or motivates her to pursue a brand new dream.

Discover the joy of collage-making as part of your own dream journey at:
www.DreamCollageArt.com

www.ingramcontent.com/pod-product-compliance
Lightning Source LLC
Chambersburg PA
CBHW051204220526
45473CB00003B/892